Beyond the Conscious Mind

The Magic of Hypnosis

Learn to use hypnosis in your everyday life to achieve results you never thought possible. Start living your dreams with the power of your unconscious mind, and the power of self-hypnosis.

Table of Contents

Chapter 5:

This book is dedicated to my wife, Connie, who day by day successfully helps people achieve their goals through hypnosis.

This book is intended to inspire all who read it to master self-hypnosis and to create a life that fulfils their dreams.

"When you change how you think, how you think changes you." – C. Michael Brannan

Beyond the Conscious Mind: The Magic of Hypnosis

Introduction

Welcome to one of the most important books you will ever read! This book can be the key to the kingdom of your heart's desires. These lessons teach you how to communicate with your unconscious mind and to take control of your feelings, your beliefs, your attitudes, your motivations and everything else over which your mind has control—which is just about everything.

Negative self-talk bothering you? Limiting beliefs stopping you from going to the next level in your business, personal life or self-development? Take control, live a life where you are in charge of your own destiny. Live a life of positive choice. This book will show you exactly how to accomplish that and so much more.

Enjoy, and if you have any questions or comments, visit my website at http://www.hypnosistraininglab.com and let me know your comments.

Chapter One: The Magic of Hypnosis

What is hypnosis?

So, what is hypnosis, and what can hypnosis do for you? The word "hypnosis" is defined by different people in many different ways, but there are some common elements to most of the common ways of understanding hypnosis.

The word "hypnosis" is derived from the Greek word "hypno" meaning "sleep", and hypnosis is often regarded as a kind of sleep. Many people think hypnosis is associated with relaxation. Yet, hypnosis is not sleep and is not always associated with relaxation. You can be quite active while in a hypnotic trance. Perhaps you've seen stage hypnosis shows where the subjects are up dancing, singing and moving quite actively. Yet, they're all in a state of deep hypnotic trance.

What they've done is use their imagination to create an alternate world. A world in which they really are Elvis Presley. Or, they are the world's greatest singing group, or they are the world's greatest spy.

Many think of hypnosis as an altered state of consciousness. It is a state of mind altered from your ordinary, conscious awareness of things. Consciously, you can be aware of only a few things going on around you. In your normal, conscious state, you respond to people talking to you. In your normal, conscious state, when you are driving, you recognize when your car is near your exit, and move to the correct lane to get on it. In your normal, conscious state, you remember driving home from work, you remember stopping at the stop lights.

When you go into an altered state of mind, none of these things may happen. You may be completely absorbed in a television show, and simply not hear what is said to you. You may drive right by your exit with no awareness of it, or you may drive all the way home, get home, and wonder how you got there. These are all common experiences and are examples of everyday hypnotic states.

One definition of hypnosis is that it is a focused attention on a single idea. James Braid, an early pioneer in the field of hypnosis, tried to rename hypnosis as "monoideaism." It's a mouthful of a word that never caught on. But it means "one idea." It focuses on one aspect of hypnosis, that the hypnotized subject is completely absorbed by a single idea. When the conscious mind is focused on a single idea, suggestions can more easily be given to the unconscious mind. You'll sometimes hear this explicitly as when the hypnotist instructs the people on stage to "focus only on the sound of my voice."

Another common definition says that hypnosis is a way to bypass the conscious mind so that you can communicate with your unconscious mind. This definition really depends on the distinction between the conscious and the unconscious mind. There are many other definitions of hypnosis. But no matter what the definition of hypnosis, most regard hypnosis as a special state of mind in which it is easier for you to accept suggestions, and to make changes in thought and behavior that can really improve your life.

It is an incredibly powerful method for self-development in almost everything you do. It can be used to improve your relationships with your family, improve your productivity, improve your creativity, improve your sports performance and much more. It can be used to end bad habits, whether those are bad eating habits, smoking or finger nail biting. It can help to end unreasonable fears and many more things.

In hypnosis, you can learn new things at an incredible rate. This is why children absorb so much information so quickly: they are in a permanent state of hypnosis during the early years of their lives. They have not yet developed a "critical factor;" they simply accept what they are told.

At *Mindworks Hypnosis & NLP,* we say that hypnosis is a state of accelerated, unconscious learning, and we are the first to characterize hypnosis in this way.

This characterization gets past the particular way the mind might enter this state (by focusing on a single idea or by other methods), and puts emphasis on the positive effect of the state of mind. It is a state of mind where learning can be instant, permanent and transformative. Feelings, beliefs, attitudes and behaviors can change instantly, because the mind learns new feelings, beliefs, attitudes and more that create more positive responses for you. It is this new *learning state* that makes such incredible changes possible.

In this state, you can understand new things and learn new behaviors that help you make changes in your life. We all know times we've learned things quickly and easily. That was a hypnotic learning state.

When you enter a state of accelerated learning, you can learn new habits, adopt new beliefs, adopt new feelings, and adopt new attitudes about yourself, about other people and about the world. These new attitudes affect how you behave in the world, affect the things that you do and how you do them. When you learn to do the things that you want to do quickly and easily through hypnosis, you find adopting new habits very, very easy. That's what hypnosis is all about.

Hypnosis is about learning on an unconscious level. Things often just seem to "pop" into your conscious mind spontaneously. We've recovered lost objects with hypnosis. The most common kind of experience is that you just find yourself looking for the object somewhere (usually somewhere you know "it's not there" or somewhere you looked before), and just find it. It often doesn't rise to the level of conscious thought.

What does it feel like to be hypnotized?

 Hypnosis is a completely natural and common state of mind. You go into and out of hypnosis every day of your life, so it feels like it's perfectly normal, because it is. Watching television or reading

an engaging book can all be hypnotic. Who hasn't tried to rouse the attention of someone completely engrossed in some activity? It's sometimes really hard to get their attention.

Have you ever driven right by your exit while you were thinking about something else? Have you ever "lost track of time" and what seemed like 10-15 minutes was actually an hour or more? Have you ever driven home and then just didn't remember the drive? Maybe you even wondered if you really stopped at the stop light? Have you ever put something down and then forgotten where you put it? These are all examples of hypnotic phenomena. We become so focused on a single idea that everything else just gets shoved aside.

What does it feel like to be hypnotized? Just take a moment to relax and close your eyes for a few seconds. Then open them. Or imagine lying in bed some lazy Sunday morning with nowhere to go and nothing to do. Just lying there, relaxed, and letting your mind drift. That's what it feels like to be hypnotized. There is nothing "other worldly" or "zonked out" about the experience. It is completely normal and natural. Almost everyone finds hypnosis incredibly relaxing and peaceful.

Utilizing self-hypnosis, by giving yourself a few simple suggestions, you can emerge from trance feeling alert, refreshed, full of energy and ready for the day. If you use hypnosis at the end of the day, you can just give yourself the opposite suggestions, that when you emerge from trance, you will feel ready for a good night's sleep. That you'll go to sleep quickly and easily and will awaken refreshed, alert and full of energy.

Improved sleep can be achieved with hypnosis, and think of all the benefits you can have from just a good night's sleep. That, and so much more, lies in allowing yourself to really communicate with your unconscious mind.

History of Hypnosis

 Hypnosis has been used for over 2000 years. Egyptian sleep temples were healing, hypnotic temples, where priests would take people into hypnotic trances for the purpose of rapid healing. Some of the inductions (methods of entry into hypnotic trance) are recognizable as hypnotic inductions to this day!

Hypnosis continued to be used from the time of the ancient Egyptians to the time of the Greeks and through the Romans, the Middle Ages and up to the present time. It achieved differing levels of acceptance during the centuries from the Egyptians to modern times. Unfortunately, this powerful tool for change and self-improvement remains shrouded in fear, suspicion and skepticism in our own age.

Hypnotism has always been shrouded in mystery. Practiced only by priests in ancient Egypt or other selected groups in centuries up to now, its utility has only recently started making its way into the mainstream. Hypnotists continue to battle the academic world, which pretends that techniques cannot work unless academia has a theory for them, or unless they invented them! Don't let them fool you, don't let them stop you from doing something incredible, something that can help you get everything you truly want in life faster and easier than you ever thought possible.

The modern history of hypnotism starts with Anton Mesmer (1734-1815), and has suffered a difficult history since then. Mesmer achieved fame throughout Europe in the 1700's for his novel methods used to heal. He toured Europe demonstrating his method to thousands, and achieved spectacular therapeutic results. His fame spread throughout the European world.

The terms "mesmerism" and "mesmerized" continue in common usage to this date and show the influence Mesmer has had on the development of hypnosis. Mesmer believed that he could transfer a kind of "animal magnetism" to help people heal.

Mesmer's fame grew to such an extent that a Royal Commission was set up in France to examine Mesmer's methods and claims. Members of the commission included such notables as Benjamin Franklin, Antonie Lavosier, and John Guillotine. Unfortunately for Mesmer, the commission decided he was a fraud because they could not discover any fluid transferring between Mesmer and his subjects.

The commission set up to evaluate Mesmer's claims decided that it was essentially a fraud and the effects that he was creating had nothing to do with animal magnetism. In part, they concluded that any beneficial effects were the result of self-suggestion. How the history of hypnotism may have changed if they had followed up on that idea! But what the commission did not do, others would. It is now understood that Mesmer's success resulted from the use of suggestions and hand passes (now called "mesmeric passes" and used by hypnotists to this day). The suggestions and hand passes created a trance state, and suggestions for healing resulted in just that— healing.

Hypnosis survived into the present day largely through the work of stage hypnosis. Stage hypnosis carried on the tradition of hypnotic inductions demonstrating the power of the mind to create alternate or parallel realities.

The healing use of hypnosis has always been regarded as suspect. Even today many medical and psychological experts have rejected hypnosis as an effective way to help people make changes that they want to make. They'd rather you spend years talking about your childhood, your parents and whatnot, rather than help you make the changes you want to make, quickly and easily.

It's not their fault, though. They are doing what they were taught to do, and what they teach others to do. The way they do their work has become an unconscious habit, passed down from one generation of therapists to the next. It's a slow process to see them change, adopting more effective ways of creating change. It's almost like a "generational phobia." We once had a client who had a phobia of spiders. She learned the phobia from her mother, who had learned it from her mother! Our client started seeing the phobia in her daughter and decided 3 generations of a spider phobia was enough. Her phobia was gone in just a single session of hypnosis. Perhaps it is time for "talk therapists" to realize that enough is enough as well and move on to more effective modes of therapy.

Stage hypnosis shows and Hollywood have given a lot of false impressions about what hypnosis is. Hollywood, or "Hollyweird," as we like to say, furthered a lot of myths about hypnosis, and sometimes these myths prevent people from coming in and using hypnosis to make the changes beneficial to them.

Myths of Hypnosis

Hypnosis has been shrouded in mystery, misunderstanding and fear for centuries. Some of the myths are part of the culture, handed down from person to person based on absolutely nothing other than fears. Television shows, movies and popular cultural continue to exploit the fear that people have for hypnosis. This only reinforces the popular misconceptions of hypnosis that continue to generate fear.

So, what are some of the myths of hypnosis?

I'll Become a Mindless Robot if I'm Hypnotized

 One of the biggest myths is that you lose control when you're in hypnosis. This just isn't true. When hypnotized, you remain in full control of your faculties, have awareness of what's going on, and can reject suggestions or even emerge yourself from trance. You are aware of everything going on around you, hear the voices of the hypnotist and the other sounds around you. Think about stage shows: the stage volunteers must hear everything the hypnotist says in order to carry out the suggestions.

Stage shows perhaps help along this misconception about hypnosis, but mostly because of a misunderstanding of what really happens during a stage show. You see, in a stage show subjects are volunteering to go on stage and perform various hypnotic skits. The stage volunteers have all seen or at least heard about what is expected in a stage show. They volunteer, wanting to do the skits. They want to be the stars, they want to show off, they want to be the life of the party. It's hardly surprising how well they usually carry out the skits. It's a good excuse for doing what they want to do anyway: "I couldn't help it, I was hypnotized!"

I once attended a stage show in Las Vegas. Prior to the show the hypnotist showed on screens various suggestions. Some suggestions were common ideas of stage hypnotists' suggestions, things like "bark like a dog," or "cluck like a chicken" that are rarely used today (if they ever were). Even though there was absolutely no hypnosis involved, 15 or 20% of the audience still followed the "bark like a dog" suggestion and started making barking sounds. You see, the people were there to have fun and to perform. They are happy and willing to do things on stage that they may never otherwise get a chance to do. It's fun for the volunteers, and if weren't fun, they wouldn't volunteer. I can't count the number of people I've seen who volunteer again and again to go on stage for a stage show.

To the audience however it may seem that the subjects are acting against their will, and doing things that they wouldn't otherwise do. In fact, however, they are doing exactly what they volunteered to do.

Hypnosis Will Make Me Tell All My Secrets

Another myth of hypnosis is that hypnosis is a truth serum and you will reveal all of your deepest, darkest secrets. Nothing could be further from the truth. A hypnotized subject may lie, may remain silent or tell the truth as they choose. Many stage shows will have one of the hypnotized volunteers lie about something. The skit may have one of the subjects pretend to be a secret agent, and when the hypnotists ask him about what he's doing, he'll lie about it as any good secret agent would.

I Wasn't Hypnotized—I Heard Everything You Said

Some people think that when they're hypnotized they won't be able to hear or understand what's going on around them. In fact, under hypnosis, your senses are much more heightened than they are normally. You hear more, see more, and are more aware of your surroundings than you are in a normal conscious state.

The reason for that is that, in hypnosis, your conscious mind is bypassed and is not interfering with your perceptions. It's not filtering out things that it normally would. That's why stage hypnotists always want the audience to be completely silent when they hypnotize the volunteers. Whispers or conversations in the audience can sound quite loud to the volunteers and can stop them from going into a deep trance.

Hypnotherapy clients will sometimes think they weren't hypnotized because they "heard everything."

Of course, they heard everything. The session wouldn't be of much use if the client didn't hear what the hypnotherapist said!

In truth, you will hear and be aware of everything going on around you, and you will likely remember everything as well. A hypnotherapist may sometimes deliberately create amnesia in a client for some specific reason, but amnesia is certainly not an automatic result of being hypnotized.

Only the Weak Minded Can Be Hypnotized

Another myth of hypnosis is that only the weak minded can be hypnotized. Nothing could be further from the truth. To go into a deep hypnotic trance requires a creative use of your imagination, your intelligence, and your ability to concentrate. In fact, the more intelligent you are, the more you're willing to use your ability to imagine and concentrate, the easier it will be to go into a deep hypnotic trance. The only thing stopping you from going into a trance is you.

Many people choose not to go into a trance because they believe one of the myths about hypnosis. When you get past the myths and really decide to "go for it" you'll find hypnosis very easy to achieve. In fact, it is a completely normal and natural state that we all go into every day.

If I'm Hypnotized, I Might Never Wake Up

Some people are afraid of hypnosis because they fear they will never "wake up" from trance. Millions and millions of people have been hypnotized and every single one of them has emerged from trance. If a hypnotist was simply to leave the room and leave you alone you would emerge from trance all on your own. If you were tired before you got hypnotized, you might drift off to sleep and wake up after a good rest.

The best way to experience hypnosis is simply to let go of all those fears, those old concerns that held you back from experiencing a wonderful state of relaxation and accelerated learning.

In this book, we will show you how to enter a deep state of hypnotic trance, give yourself positive suggestions for achieving your goals, and emerge yourself from trance feeling alert, refreshed, feeling absolutely wonderful in every way. Hypnosis is simple and easy. You don't need to spend long periods of time to get wonderful results. You can spend as little as five minutes a day to be well on your way to achieving your own goals, the goals that you have decided are important to you.

What can hypnosis be used for?

Hypnosis can be used for almost anything. We have a saying at Mindworks Hypnosis & NLP: "If it involves the brain, hypnosis can help!" Pretty much everything you want to do involves your brain. Hypnosis has been used for everything from pain relief, to losing weight, to smoking cessation, to sports improvement, to improving study habits and many, many other things. There is really no end to what it can be used for. You are limited only by your imagination.

Here is a partial list of some of the things that hypnosis has been used for:

1. weight control
2. smoking cessation
3. pain control
4. childbirth
5. stress release
6. accelerated learning
7. improved memory
8. improved confidence
9. improved relationships
10. improved golf
11. improved basketball
12. overcoming negative fears
13. changing negative beliefs
14. acquiring new beliefs that help you achieve your goals
15. much, much more....

You get the idea—if it involves the brain, hypnosis can help you with it. The reason is that hypnosis is a way to communicate with your unconscious mind. It is your unconscious mind that controls your behavior, keeps habits going, breaks habits and learns incredibly fast.

Hypnosis has a better success rate for many of these things than other types of "help" including counseling or the use of drugs. What's more, hypnosis has absolutely no side effects, whereas drugs often have serious side effects, including death.

Advantages of Using Hypnosis

Hypnosis crushes other methods of self-development in terms of its overall effectiveness, usefulness and simplicity. Hypnosis has been used for centuries to improve health, to improve performance in all aspects of life, to relieve stress and anxiety, to end bad habits and to end phobias. During the 19th century, hypnosis was used as the only anesthesia in hundreds of painless amputations and other medical procedures. It is used today for painless, natural childbirth and to speed the recovery time after operations. The list is almost endless.

Unlike drugs, hypnosis has no negative side effects.

When you read labels on so many drugs, the potential side effects are incredible—anything from kidney failure, liver failure and more. Even depression or thoughts of suicide. It is rather alarming when you read that one potential side effect of an anti-depressant is thoughts of suicide. On the other hand, hypnosis has no negative side effects. You can tell yourself how you want to feel when you emerge from trance, and reliably feel exactly as you have told yourself.

Hypnosis works fast.

Perhaps you know someone who has "been in therapy for years," and is still waiting for the change that will likely never happen. In hypnosis, we do not attempt so much to uncover and endlessly analyze the "why" of a bad habit or some other behavior. Rather, we work directly to change the behavior to something more desirable.

Using hypnosis, we are interested in you getting what you want, not an endless and generally unproductive investigation into "why?" Understanding what motivates a behavior can, of course, be quite useful. Knowing what a person thinks and feels right before engaging in a behavior can be useful as well. But an academic inquiry into "why" is not always the most productive approach to fast and lasting change work. You just don't need to know why the dishes are dirty in order to wash them. They're dirty, you want them clean: wash them.

For example, my wife used to have a spider phobia. She knew the exact moment in her childhood when she developed the phobia and exactly how the phobia arose. It didn't help to change it one bit. What helped was teaching her brain a new way of responding to spiders other than fear and panic. When her brain learned a new response, the phobia was gone and has been gone for over 11 years now. We have gotten the same result countless times in our own hypnosis clinical work.

Suggestibility Tests

It's time to start the hypnosis! In this section, we'll introduce you to some "suggestibility tests," and give you a method of self-hypnosis. The tests really show the connection between the mind and the body, and that what happens in the mind can have obvious effects on what happens in the body.

The psychology literature has shown that the brain cannot really distinguish between something that is vividly imagined and reality. We'll illustrate that with the first suggestibility test. You can experiment with this yourself, just use your powers of imagination and creativity to get the right effect.

The suggestibility tests here are standard in the hypnotic literature. They are quick, easy and illustrate how your mind works. Go ahead and experiment with them yourself.

Lemon Test

Imagine a nice firm lemon in your hand. Feel the weight of the lemon, feel it as though it is really there. Notice the weight, the texture of the skin, breathe in through your nose as you smell that special scent of the lemon. Imagine you are cutting the lemon open, exposing the nice, juicy insides of this wonderful, fresh smelling lemon. Imagine you are holding the lemon up to your nose—that's right, bring your hand to your nose, and take a nice deep breath through your nose as you continue to feel its weight and texture, see its juices running out. Take a bite, imagining how it is to taste it now.

Now that you've read the directions, experiment with it. When you do, you'll notice that you mouth waters, that you can smell and taste the lemon, even though there is really no lemon there. Cool, huh?

Your mind can create an experience for you exactly as if the lemon were there!

Finger Vice Experiment

Here is another suggestibility test, and if you've ever gone to a stage show, you've likely seen this one in action. Interlace your fingers and clasp your hands together, palm against palm. Squeeze your hands together, and then raise the index finger of each hand. The fingers should be separated by at least an inch.

Look steadily and directly between your two fingers.

Now, imagine magnets are in each finger, pulling the fingers together. It's like there is a vice closing, driving the fingers together, closer and closer…closer and closer. The vice tightens, or the magnets grow stronger and stronger, pulling your fingers closer and closer together.

Now that you've read the directions, experiment with it. Try it with your friends. Just go through the set up and give suggestions of the fingers drawing closer and closer together, that they are being drawn together as if powerful magnets are pulling the fingers together. Notice how fast the fingers start closing together.

Chapter 2: The Conscious and Unconscious Mind

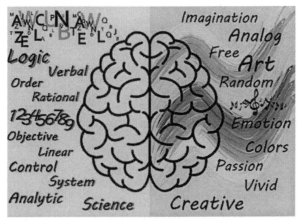

The first part of this book talked about hypnosis, what it is, how it feels and some history. We've demolished the myths of hypnosis so you know hypnosis is safe and effective. You know that hypnosis works with your unconscious mind, the storehouse of habits, beliefs and attitudes. You've learned that by changing these, you can propel yourself forward—you can eliminate bad habits, get good ones and acquire mindsets that propel you to the next level and beyond.

Next, you'll learn all about the conscious and unconscious mind, and self-hypnosis. You'll learn how to take yourself into a hypnotic trance and how to use that trance to start making positive changes. You'll see just how pleasant and relaxing the trance experience can be, and you'll be excited to go on to learn more about hypnosis, and everything you can do with it. You'll learn how to hypnotize yourself for positive changes and start on the road to complete self-mastery.

The Conscious and the Unconscious Mind

Hypnosis is sometimes defined as "bypassing the critical factor." The critical factor is really the conscious mind, which acts as a "gatekeeper" to keep out suggestions that don't already agree with what's going on in your mind.

That's why it is difficult, sometimes, to get affirmations to work: you repeat them and repeat them, but the conscious mind, the gatekeeper, does not allow them to embed into your unconscious mind, where real change happens. The "gatekeeper" filters out the suggestions because they are incompatible with what you already believe. This is often extremely useful: you don't want to take onboard every negative suggestion someone gives you or be unduly influenced by advertisements.

Hypnosis works on the unconscious mind. The unconscious mind ultimately controls your behavior: it is the storehouse of habits, of motivation, of your life's memory and so much more. It controls all the involuntary actions of your body—it regulates your heartbeat, your body temperature, your blood pressure, and virtually everything else that your body does. When we have effective communication with the unconscious mind, these things can be altered to some extent.

So, what's the difference between the conscious and the unconscious mind? The conscious mind is very limited. In one well recognized psychological study conducted by George Miller in 1955, the conscious mind can only hold 7 plus/minus 2 bits of information at a time (short term memory). That's not very much. The unconscious mind, however, is nearly unlimited— it processes millions of bits of information at every moment of time.

The difference between the conscious and the unconscious mind has been compared to the difference between a peanut and the entire planet!

Permanent, lasting change happens when you change the unconscious, when you adopt new habits, beliefs and attitudes that propel you to your goal.

When you create goals and visions that truly drive your unconscious mind, achieving your goals becomes almost automatic. Hypnosis is the most effective method known to do just that. You start noticing the things you need to notice to become successful and taking the actions you need to take become automatic and habitual.

The conscious mind is analytical, logical and sequential. It thinks of one thing at a time and then thinks of the next thing, and then the next thing and so forth. It is our thinking mind. The unconscious is unlimited and expansive. It can take in entire collections of information all at once. It processes a multitude of information all at once.

It's why you can make quick decisions about things, whether you like someone or don't, whether something is a good idea or not: your unconscious mind processes all the cues and signals of which you aren't consciously aware and directs an action.

The conscious mind is logical and deliberate. It's the part of your brain that gets racked when you rack your brain. The unconscious mind, on the other hand, knows solutions to problems that we cannot consciously solve (if we could consciously solve them, we would have done so already!). The unconscious mind is the feeling part of your mind (all emotions are in the unconscious mind). It is responsible for involuntary movements, it keeps our hearts pumping blood, our lungs breathing and all the other automatic responses that keep us alive. The unconscious mind responds: you don't have to think about a joke to start laughing. You just "get it" and respond. Jokes tend not to be so funny when you must "think about it" to get the joke.

Formal hypnosis, whether self-induced or induced by another person, is only one way to communicate with the unconscious mind. Relaxing and letting your unconscious mind guide small muscle movement is another, and it is easy to demonstrate that effect.

Self-Hypnosis

One of the best ways to experience hypnosis is through self-hypnosis, which I explain shortly. There are many, many ways to take yourself into hypnotic trance, and to fire off positive suggestions to help you eliminate bad habits, overcome fears, improve confidence, improve learning, memory and much, much more.

When you first start with hypnosis, just practice going into trance; there is no need to give yourself real suggestions right away. Just tell yourself that you are going into hypnosis for 5 minutes to refresh and relax your mind, and when you emerge, you will feel wonderful, energized and ready to face the rest of the day.

If you're using self-hypnosis before you go to sleep at night, you can give yourself a different suggestion for emerging—that you will emerge fully ready for a good, nighttime sleep and will awake in the morning feeling refreshed and ready for the day ahead.

To start, stay with these suggestions, and as you progress and learn how to frame suggestions, you can make them more involved, and more directed towards the things you want to accomplish with hypnosis.

One easy way to learn self-hypnosis is to have a good hypnotist take you into trance and give you a key phrase or action that takes you back into trance instantly. This is one of the techniques we use in our clinical work at Mindworks Hypnosis & NLP, http://www.mindworkshypnosis.net. I have included an audio of a hypnosis session that does just that.

Find a comfortable place where you can relax and listen to the audio. It takes you into a hypnotic trance, and gives you cue words that will return you to that state of mind, or even deeper, each and every time you say the trigger words to yourself when you have the intention of going into trance. Obviously, only use the words when it is safe and appropriate to do so—when you can comfortably relax for a few minutes. Do not use the recording when driving, operating machinery or anything else that may require your attention.

The Betty Erickson Induction

The Betty Erickson Induction is one popular technique for self-hypnosis. It is easy to do, and produces a good, working trance in a short time. It illustrates the difference, so important to hypnosis, of an inward focus of attention and an outward focus of attention.

Get Comfortable

Find a place where you will not be disturbed, a comfortable chair to sit on or a place to lie down for the session. Breathe slowly and easily, in through the nose and out through the mouth, slowly, easily and evenly. Relax your body and mind.

Decide on a length of time for hypnosis

When you just start out practicing hypnosis, five minutes is enough. At that point, you are learning how to go into hypnosis. It is a learning process, and the more you do it, the better you will become. You'll go into trance deeper, faster and with incredible results. You can extend the time when you start giving yourself suggestions for change.

Say how you want to feel when you come out of trance

Give yourself a suggestion for how you want to feel when you come out of trance. If you practice at the start of the day, you might suggest "When I come out of trance, I feel energized, positive, and confident that I achieve the things I choose to do for the day." If you are practicing before you go to sleep, you might suggest "When I come out of trance, I feel relaxed, comfortable and ready for a good night's rest."

State what you want

I go over with you how to frame a goal properly later in this chapter. For now, when you go into hypnosis you can suggest to yourself "I am going into self-hypnosis for 5 minutes for practicing self-hypnosis."

When I talk about actual suggestions for change, I'll explain how to form suggestions for positive change.

Once you've said out loud or to yourself how you want to feel when you come out of trance and stated your goal, you're ready to hypnotize yourself. You'll see that nothing could really be easier.

The Betty Erickson Process

External Process

First, with your eyes open, look at three physical things in your environment one at a time. Look at each item, pausing for a short while on each item, noticing everything you can about it. Look at small things, like a spot on the wall, a doorknob, a candle, an item on a table, etc. Some people like to name the items as they look at them. As you look at each of the objects, focus all your attention on the objects, keeping your mind as free from random thoughts as possible. If you mind does wander, that's fine, just bring it back to the object you are looking at.

Second, pay attention to three things that you hear, one at a time. It may be the sound of a fan, the music from outside, the sound of your own breathing, or anything else you hear. Focus on it, noticing as much about it as you can in a short time. If your mind starts to wander, bring it back to what you're attending to.

Third, pay attention to three things that you feel, paying special attention to things that might normally be outside of your attention. This might be things like the weight of your shoes on your feet, the feeling of the air on your skin, the feeling of your watch on your wrist, or the feeling of your socks against your feet.

Repeat this same cycle with two things you see, two things you hear and two things that you feel.

After repeating the cycle with two things, repeat it with one thing you see, one thing you hear and one thing you feel.

You may have felt like closing your eyes long before you complete the process. That's fine, just close your eyes when you feel ready—it is a sign that you are dropping into a good level of trance. When you've closed your eyes, go to the internal portion of the process, next, whether you have completed the external part or not.

If you made it this far into the process without going into trance, the next portion of the process will take you into trance. You have completed the external portion of the process, you now begin the internal portion. If your eyes have not already closed, close them now. If your eyes closed before you completed the external portion of the process, leave them closed and begin the internal portion of the process.

Internal Process

This is like the external portion of the process, but is done with things you see, hear and feel in your imagination, in your mind. But instead of going from three things to one, we reverse, going from one thing to three. It is likely that you will go into a deep trance long before your finish the entire process.

First, imagine one thing that you could see. Anything, a book, a street scene, your friend's face! See it in your mind's eye, keeping your eyes closed. Focus on it for a short while, noticing everything about it.

Second, imagine one thing that you could hear such as the sound of a bird chirping, a car, or a few notes of a song. Focus on this one sound for a moment, noticing as much as you can about it before going on.

Third, imagine one thing that you could feel, such as the warmth of the sun on your skin or the texture of your hair. Focus on it for a moment, noticing as much about it as possible.

Repeat this process with two different imagined images, two different imagined sounds and two different imagined feelings.

Repeat the cycle once again using three different images, three different sounds and three different feelings.

Anytime you are struggling to continue the process, just let it go, knowing that you have already achieved a good level of trance, a level of trance good enough to be able to create significant changes in your feelings, beliefs, actions and habits.

This is the basics of the Betty Erickson induction. It has been used by countless individuals to take themselves into a good, working state of self-hypnosis. When combined with the method for giving yourself suggestions explained later, it will provide an incredibly powerful way of making changes in your mind and body and life.

Progressive Relaxation

A progressive **relaxation induction** is probably one of the most common hypnotic inductions, or methods of entering trance. If you have seen a stage show, the hypnotist probably used this kind of induction. You can also use it on yourself.

As the name suggests, a progressive relaxation induction takes you through a series of steps in which you completely relax each of your major muscle groups, from the tips of your toes to the top of your head (some go the other direction—experiment to find out which way seems best for you. In the example below, I start at the tips of your toes, and move to the top of your head.

Go through the same initial process that you did with the Betty Erickson induction. It is stated here again for convenience:

Get Comfortable

Find a place where you will not be disturbed, a comfortable chair to sit on or a place to lie down for the session. Breathe slowly and easily, in through the nose and out through the mouth, slowly, easily and evenly. Relax your body and mind.

Decide on a length of time for hypnosis

When you start out practicing, five minutes is enough. At that point, you are learning how to go into hypnosis. It is a learning process, and the more you do it, the better you will become. You'll go into trance deeper, faster and with incredible results. You can extend the time when you start giving yourself suggestions for change.

Say how you want to feel when you come out of trance

Give yourself a suggestion for how you want to feel when you come out of trance. If you practice at the start of the day, you might suggest "When I come out of trance, I feel energized, positive, and confident that I achieve the things I choose to do for the day." If you are practicing before you go to sleep, you might suggest "When I come out of trance, I feel relaxed, comfortable and ready for a good night's rest.

State what you want

I go over with you how to frame a goal properly later. For now, when you go into hypnosis you can suggest to yourself "I am going into self-hypnosis for 5 minutes for practicing self-hypnosis." When I talk about actual suggestions for change, I'll explain how to form suggestions for positive change.

Once you have done these simple techniques, use the progressive relaxation induction to take yourself into trance. You can initially repeat your self-suggestion as you relax each of the muscle groups when you start. After a short time of practice, you'll find that you go into a good level of hypnotic trance in just a couple of minutes.

I include this induction here and a version of the progressive relaxation induction is used in the audio induction included with this book.

Progressive Relaxation Induction

Breathe slowly, easily and comfortably, in through your nose and out through your mouth, allowing your whole body to relax quickly and easily.

Focus your attention on your toes, the little muscles in your toes and feet, allowing them to relax completely. Feel the relaxation moving through every nerve, every muscle, every fiber in your toes and feet. Count down from 3 to 1 relaxing your toes and feet more and more completely as you count.

Move your attention to your calf muscles, letting them relax. Let your shins and knees relax, feel the relaxation in your muscles as you see your muscles become loose and limp, perhaps even hearing soft and relaxing sounds. Count down from 3 to 1 relaxing every muscle and nerve in your body even more.

Move your attention to your thighs and the back of your legs, relaxing each muscle totally and completely as you continue to breathe in deep relaxation; every breath allows you to relax more and more. Relax those muscles completely, feel those muscles become loose and limp. You may count down from 3 to 1 allowing those muscles to relax even more completely, every muscle, every nerve, every fiber relaxing more deeply.

Continue to move to your buttocks, relaxing completely; you entirely body drifting in a state of wonderful relaxation now, so completely relaxed, feeling those warm, comfortable waves of relaxation moving through your body, each deep, easy breath relaxing you more.

Focus now on your stomach, relaxing those muscles completely. Notice how good it feels to just relax. Move to your chest, relaxing completely, paying

*attention to the comfort and relaxation that you have
already achieved, so quickly, so easily.*

*Relax your back now, completely. Every nerve, every
muscle, every fiber of your being, so completely
relaxed, so completely comfortable. Now, focus on
your fingers and hands, relaxing them completely and
totally, feeling so good, so comfortable. Move up,
relaxing your arms, your shoulders, your neck, your
face and your head. Breathe deeply, evenly, allowing
your breath to relax you even more deeply.*

Now that you have completely relaxed, just let your
mind drift and wander as you continue to focus on
your breathing. You have already stated to your
unconscious mind the purpose of the self-hypnosis,
so just let your unconscious mind do the work. You
will just relax in this nice, pleasant state for the length
of time you decided and will come out of trance
feeling just the way you suggested to yourself that
you would.

Once you practice this technique, you will be able to
completely relax your entire body in a matter of
seconds. How good will you feel when you are able to

so completely relax, so quickly and achieve amazing outcomes as a result?

Chapter 3: Your Goals ~ Your Mind

 In the previous chapter, we discussed the distinction between the conscious and unconscious mind. We explained how the unconscious mind is the root of all your habits, beliefs, emotions and other drivers in your life. We also explained how hypnosis bypasses the conscious mind and works with the unconscious mind to help you make changes that you want to make.

We introduced you to two methods for inducing self-hypnosis: the Betty Erickson induction and a progressive relaxation induction. You also have an audio of a progressive relaxation induction that gives you a trigger word to induce trance. Use them.

Of course, once you are in hypnosis, you will have to know how to make good goals for yourself and how to make good, effective suggestions for yourself. This chapter explains goal setting for you.

Goal Setting

To use hypnosis, you must first decide on a goal or outcome that you want to achieve. The goal might be to lose 20 lbs in 8 weeks, or to become a complete non-smoker. It might a goal for improved memory or concentration, reduced stress or any number of other possible goals.

Follow the rules given here and you will be able to form a good goal for yourself. One that you can use with the power of hypnosis, the power of your own mind, to achieve.

Elements of a Well-Formed Goal

Forming a Good Goal: *State Your Goal in the Positive*

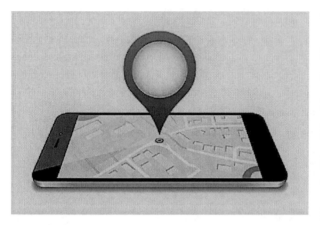 Your goal should be stated in the positive. You can think of your unconscious mind as a GPS: if you give your GPS a destination, it will give you directions to that destination. What would happen if you just told your GPS "I don't want to go to the library?" You won't end up at the library, but who knows where you will end up. Maybe the garbage dump. But the chance of ending up where you want to go is nearly zero.

The same thing happens when you do not state your goals in the positive. If you frame a goal as "I don't want to feel stress," your unconscious mind does not know how you do want to feel. Do you want to feel angry? Hateful? Depressed? Form your goal in a completely positive frame, and your unconscious mind, like a good GPS, will take you there.

Forming a Good Goal: *State Your Goal in an Appropriate Context*

Your goal should be put in an appropriate context. Most goals have a specific place and time when you want it, when it would be appropriate. For example, there will be a time and a place where you want to feel more confident, but probably not everyplace. Few of us want to feel confident in doing brain surgery with a fork and knife. You may want to feel confident when you're giving your next presentation at the business meeting, or you may want to feel more confident when stepping up to tee off the golf shot. Always be clear about the context of your goal: who, what, where, how, when, how and why (in the sense of what motivates you to achieve your goal).

Forming a Good Goal: *Make Your Goal Sensory Based*

Make sure you have a good sense of what you will be seeing, saying (out loud and to yourself), feeling, thinking and believing once you have achieved your goal. What will you be saying to yourself as you stand up to give your next presentation? What will you be seeing in your mind—a room full of friendly, responsive people? What will other people be saying to you and about you? Really "step into" your success so you fully imagine what it is like. That way, you will know it when you see it for real in your world. How will you measure success?

Forming a Good Goal: *Get it Done by Yourself*

Goals achieved in hypnosis are ones that you can start yourself and continue by yourself. They are things that you have control and power over by yourself, and do not depend on the actions of others. Others may change as you change, but your goal is something you can initiate and maintain by yourself. A goal like "eat healthier" is something you can initiate and maintain by yourself—you decide what food to eat. "I feel more confident when I speak in public" is a goal you can initiate and maintain by self.

Now, this doesn't mean that your overall goal will always be something you can initiate and maintain by yourself. You can have a goal of "selling $1,000,000 of real estate in the next six months." A goal like that requires someone else to do something—to buy real estate from you. A way to achieve that goal, though, may be to increase your confidence in selling real estate, which is something under your control.

Break down your goals to the aspects that are in your control and the aspects that are out of your control— use hypnosis to work on the parts that are in your control.

Forming a Good Goal: *Make Sure It Fits into the Whole of Your Life*

When you change your beliefs, feelings and attitudes, it will influence people around you. When you stop smoking, how will your relationships change with people who smoke? When you stand tall, confident at the business meeting, how will it change your relationships with your co-workers? When you drop those excess pounds, how will it change how others relate to you? Are the changes worth it to you? Think through how your change will affect your life. If the changes are what you want, go for it!

Once you have decided on your goal, the next step is to frame suggestions that will help you meet those goals. If you want to stop smoking, your goal might be

"I am a healthy non-smoker." If you want to lose weight, it might be "I make all the changes necessary in my diet and exercise to drop 1-2 lbs/week of excess weight."

In the next section, we go over how to make simple, effective suggestions for making the changes that you want to make.

Suggestions for Suggestions

To make self-hypnosis the most useful it can possibly be, there are some things good to know about how to make suggestions to yourself. What are suggestions? Simply, they are the ideas you present to your unconscious mind for fulfillment.

The first, most basic, and important rule is that the suggestions should be stated in the positive. You always state the suggestion in terms of what you want in a positive way rather that what you don't want. Many self-hypnotists just starting out state suggestions in terms of what they don't want, e.g. "I don't want to feel tired," or "I don't want to stay awake at night," or "I don't want to eat too much sugar."

None of these examples are phrased in a positive way: ok, you don't want to feel tired. How do you want to feel? Do you want to feel physically energized? Do you want to feel mentally alert? Do you want to feel well-rested? These are all different ways of "not feeling tired," but they will have different purposes. You may want to feel more physically energized when you are going to the gym. You may want to feel more mentally alert when you are going to school, but perhaps not as physically energized as when you are going to the gym. Perhaps you want to feel well rested for your routine day-to-day activities, where feeling as physically energized as you do when you go to the gym isn't as useful

You see, every activity you do will have an optimal state of body and mind that will go with that activity. A state of mind that makes doing the task easier and more efficient. You must think about how you actually want to think and feel that will allow you to do what you need to do in the best way possible.

In hypnosis, we have a lot of little sayings, a lot of little "mind cues" that keep us on track in creating suggestions. A couple of these are "where attention goes, energy flows," and "what you focus on expands."

When you think about it, when you say "I don't want to feel tired" you are focusing on feeling tired. For you to understand the sentence, you have to create some way of thinking about "being tired." The sentence doesn't tell you how to feel in any positive way like "I want to feel physically energized" does. When you focus on being tired, you will get more of being tired, exactly what you don't want.

When you focus on what you do want instead, feeling physically energized, you will get more of that, which is what you want. The mind is an amazing thing: it will give you exactly what you want, so focus your goals on the things you really want.

Rule one:

State your suggestions in the positive, stating exactly what you want, rather than what you don't want. Some examples of suggestions stated in the positive:

1. I sleep well through the night, awakening at the designated time feeling well rested and ready to successfully complete my tasks for the day.
2. My memory is perfect. I easily remember names, faces and other facts and information that I want to remember.
3. My mind and body are relaxed in exactly the way they need to be to do this task.
4. I am physically energized ready to complete my exercises in a way that improves my health quickly.
5. I am a total non-smoker. I delight in always breathing in fresh air, breathing deeply and allowing my breath to energize me and make me healthier.
6. I eat healthy foods. I enjoy eating them knowing how healthy they make me feel.

These suggestions are all stated in the positive. The only one you might wonder about is "I am a non-smoker" but that phrase has a positive meaning of its own—you can make a picture in your mind of a non-smoker without bringing smoking into it. It might be someone with rosy, healthy cheeks breathing fresh, clean air. In my picture, it's slightly cold, and you can see the breath as he exhales, knowing that breath is good health.

Rule two:

Put your suggestion in an appropriate context. Notice when we used the example of feeling "physically energized" above, we put it in a context when the suggestion is appropriate—when you're going to the gym to work out. You don't always want to feel physically energized; for instance, it would not be a useful feeling if you're settling in for sleep. Your suggestions will have a context where they are useful. You may want to feel confident and at ease when speaking in public, but maybe not so much when you're doing brain surgery with a hatchet.

Rule three:

Your suggestions to yourself should be short, simple and direct. One or, at most, two sentences is more than sufficient. What you understand with the suggestion, of course, may be more complex, but the actual suggestion should be simple. It can act as a shorthand for a longer suggestion. An example might be: "I use my memory techniques quickly and efficiently." Your suggestion doesn't need to say what the memory techniques are as you already know that. The suggestion is a shorthand way of capturing the entire suggestion. Remember, this is the suggestion you'll give yourself right before your go into hypnosis, so keep it simple.

Rule four:

State your command in a totally confident and assured manner. State your command as if it is a foregone conclusion that the outcome you want has already been achieved. It's the fastest way of making it happen. This isn't "fake it till you make it," it's about adopting the mindset that you have already achieved your goal.

These are four rules you can use in forming suggestions for yourself. The most important here is to state the suggestion as a positive thing and to put the suggestion in an appropriate context. At this point, and for the next few weeks, practice going into trance and just give yourself some simple suggestions. You might, for example, give yourself suggestions for improved memory, improved confidence or improved sleep.

The very first self-hypnotic suggestion you should give to yourself, is the suggestion to use self-hypnosis every day. It can take as little as 2-3 minutes and can be done right before bed and anytime you have a few minutes. You'll come out of trance ready for sleep if you do it at night or to be incredibly productive for the rest of the day if you do it in the morning.

Proper goal setting is an involved thing and is covered in more detail in other articles at hypnosistraininglab.com and our live trainings scheduled at Mindworks NLP, http://www.seattlenlptraining.com.

Next up, you'll learn signs of trance and phenomena of depth of trance. You'll learn how to take yourself even deeper into self-hypnosis, learn some basic self-hypnosis suggestions for common issues, and much more that unlocks the door to your inner mind.

Here is a "cheat sheet" of the process so far.

The Process to date:

Preparation Steps:

1. Get Comfortable
2. Decide on a length of time for hypnosis
3. Say how you want to feel when you come out of trance
4. State what you want (the suggestion for this particular hypnotic trance)

The Induction

1. Use one of the techniques for self-hypnosis revealed in this book
2. Let your mind drift as your unconscious activates the suggestion

Emerge

1. Emerge from trance feeling the way you instructed yourself to feel knowing that the suggestion you gave yourself is already taking deep root in your mind.

Use the "cheat sheet" above to refresh your learning as you continue your journey to hypnotic mastery.

Chapter 4: Mind/Body Connection

 In previous chapters, we learned the history of hypnosis, discussed some of the myths of hypnosis, what it feels like to be hypnotized and what hypnosis really is. You've already experienced self-hypnosis (if you're following along) either with the audio induction provided or by using one of the hypnotic inductions provided. You now realize that it is really easy to go into a hypnotic trance. You may have already experienced some positive benefits from it.

We've given you an easy method for creating good goals for yourself, goals you can use self-hypnosis to achieve, and we've given you some rules for framing good suggestions for use in hypnosis.

We now take you through the signs of trance, trance deepeners and a give you the text of a full progressive relaxation induction to enhance the shorter one we gave earlier. We go over some of the things that you can notice about yourself when you are in self-hypnosis. If you decide to take your skills to the next level and hypnotize others, knowing these "signs of trance" will be extremely useful to you.

One fact about hypnosis and why it is so effective is because of the connection between the mind and body. The mind controls the body and the body controls the mind. Change one and the other will automatically change. This is how we can change poor physical habits by influencing the mind. It is also how we can change our mental state by changing our body position.

A fun and revealing exercise

 It is easy to demonstrate this effect, and you can do it right now. Stand up like someone who is very depressed—head hanging down, shoulders slumped, a depressed expression on your face. As you take that position, you might start feeling a little depressed yourself. Now, as you maintain that body position, try to think of really happy thoughts. It's not very easy.

You can do it the other way, too. Stand up straight in perfect posture with a big smile or grin across your face, maybe even laughing a little. As you maintain that body position, try to think of something depressing. Notice how hard it is to do that.

One of the classic, and more useful, demonstrations of the mind/body connection is the pendulum described below. You can use this to access your unconscious mind to answer questions for yourself. We have used it many times to locate lost objects, just with a series of yes/no questions.

Demonstrating the Mind/Body Connection: The Pendulum

You can illustrate the mind/body connection and the possibility of communication with the unconscious mind with a **pendulum**. Attach a small weight (maybe a small stone, a bead or a bolt) to the end of a

string. Grip one end of the string between your forefinger and thumb as in the illustration below. I prefer to rest my elbow on a table when I work with a pendulum; others prefer to keep their arm freely hanging in the air. Try both and see what seems to work best for you.

When you focus on any thought, it will influence the body. How you hold your body, whether you stand straight up or slouched over, whether your hands are moving or are still, all are associated with what is going on in your brain. When you think about different things, there will always be some change in your body that will accompany that thought. That's why noticing and reading body language can be so effective. On a high enough level, reading body language is almost indistinguishable from mind reading.

The pendulum technique takes advantage of the fact that your thoughts, even your unconscious thoughts, will have a physical effect on your body.

We use the pendulum to answer yes/no questions, by setting up different motions for the pendulum when the answer to the question is "yes" or "no" or "I don't know". When the pendulum swings in one direction, it signals the unconscious response of "yes" and when it swings in a different direction, it signals the unconscious response of "no." The unconscious mind knows solutions to problems we cannot consciously solve, and has more information stored within.

How to Use the Pendulum

As you hold the pendulum in this exercise, do not attempt to make it move, but do not keep it from moving either. Just allow it to move if it does so. As you focus on "yes," small micro-movements of your muscles will cause the pendulum to move. Notice what you notice about how the pendulum moves.

There are four basic movements: left/right, forward/backwards, clockwise circle and counterclockwise. There are other possible movements, of course, such as diagonal, but these are the four ones normally found. There is no "right or wrong" movement, you will find what your unconscious mind chooses.

The first thing you want to do is establish a movement of the pendulum to mean "yes." Hold the pendulum as illustrated above and focus you mind on "yes." Repeat it in your mind the word "yes." In a few moments, the pendulum will start moving, and that will be the movement associated with a "yes" answer.

It may take a few moments for it to happen, so don't rush it. Next, follow the same procedure to establish the word "no", and then "I don't know." Once you have established movements for the pendulum for "yes,' "no" and "I don't know," you can start asking your unconscious mind questions.

Start with the pendulum resting completely still and focus on your yes/no question. In a few moments, you should see the pendulum start to move in response to your question, and that is your unconscious mind talking to you!

Ask it a few questions that you know the answer to (e.g. am I male/am I female?) and wait for an answer. Then ask questions you are less certain about, but questions that your unconscious mind may know the answer—e.g. "am I prepared for the test tomorrow?" If you don't know if your unconscious mind knows the answer to the question, ask it: "unconscious mind, do you know the answer to the question…..?" and it will tell you.

This technique is incredibly useful. We've used it to find lost objects, to figure out a good training program, select an office space and many more things. It's even useful to deciding where to go out for dinner!

Play with the pendulum, practice with this unconscious communication and see how well it works for you. There are many, many other ways to communicate with the unconscious mind that are discussed in hypnosis books such as my upcoming book on automatic writing and other hypnotic phenomena. Stay tuned!

Signs of Trance

We know from the pendulum experiment that every thought will show itself in some way in the body. When you go into hypnotic trance, there will be changes in your body as well, and there are several changes that typically go with trance. I'll go over some of those here. If you've had an opportunity to play with the self-hypnosis, you will almost certainly recognize some of these signs or trance.

One of the first, and one of the most important things to learn are signs of trance. You may notice some of these things when you take yourself into hypnosis. Some of the others you will notice if you video record your self-hypnosis session, just to see what it looks like. It's kind of fun!

What is especially interesting about the signs of trance, once you become aware of them, you start seeing them in everyone. You'll see them in your everyday interactions with other people, you may even notice some of them in yourself. There's nothing wrong with this: it just shows how commonplace these phenomena are and how easy it is for people to slip into and out of these states of mind during everyday interactions.

If you enjoy this material, we also show how to use these everyday trances to be more persuasive, more influential and more effective in your communication, through trainings provided at seattlenlptraining.com.

Signs of trance range from the obvious to the very subtle. Here are some obvious signs of trance you may experience in self-hypnosis. When we talk about the "signs of trance," we are noticing changes in your physiology that might suggest changes in your mental state as well.

1. **Relaxation of the entire body**. You might notice shoulders dropping, the chin may drop to the chest, the arms will be loose and limp.

2. **You might notice that your rate of breathing slows and your heart rate slows**

3. **You might notice your eyelids flutter or rapid movement of the eyes behind the eyelids.** This is a good sign of trance, though will not be present in a more active hypnotic state.

4. **You might notice a mask-like appearance.** As the muscles in the face relax, the face can take on a mask like or waxy expression. This is something you can see if you video record your self-hypnosis, just to get a sense of what hypnosis looks like.

5. **You might notice changes in swallowing.** The swallowing reflex may increase.

6. **You might notice changes in skin color.** Often the skin will become paler. As the heart rate goes down, blood flow is reduced, giving the skin a more pale color.

7. **You might notice a change in body temperature.** In many cases the hypnotized person might feel colder than normal, so it's always a good idea to have a blanket available when you use self-hypnosis.

8. **Other signs:** There are other signs such as watering of the eyes that you may notice. You might notice pupil dilation, a change in the rate at

which eyes blink. When you go into hypnosis, just notice what is different about the state than your normal waking state. It will serve you well as you continue to practice.

Hypnotic Inductions

 Again, an induction is simply an intentional method of taking yourself or someone else into a state of hypnosis. One of the most common hypnotic inductions is a **progressive relaxation** induction. You sampled this induction earlier. I am giving a full text of the induction, so you can record it if you would like. It will be in your own voice (we recommend that you use the word "you" rather than "I" in your commands).

A progressive relaxation induction uses certain hypnotic themes that center around relaxation, feeling relaxed, feeling comfortable, feeling secure, feeling calm, feeling at ease and other feelings that you might associate with being relaxed. A progressive relaxation induction will use these words to help bring a deep state of trance.

In addition to these themes, the relaxation induction will associate feeling relaxed, etc. with going deep into trance. There is a kind of cultural knowledge and expectation regarding what trance is supposed to be, and we can use that expectation to connect the words of relaxation in the induction with going into trance.

A second element of a progressive relaxation induction is motivation. It is important to give a reason to go into trance. Many inductions will associate relaxation and trance with feeling good, e.g. "the deeper you go, the better you feel as you continue to relax more and feel more and more comfortable." See how the elements can be easily put together.

If you are working on a specific issue (some improvement in your life or some problem you want to solve), you can connect achieving your goal with going deeply into trance, e.g. "As you relax even more and feel more comfortable, your unconscious mind is already learning how to make the changes you want, and the deeper you go, the more your unconscious mind makes these changes." This is a more advanced technique as it merges the induction with the change work. Though we mention it here, you will find that this technique not widely known, even among professional hypnotists.

There are, of course, many additional elements to an induction that are beyond the scope of this book. By noticing how you respond to the inductions and the specific techniques, you can make enormous progress very quickly in your mastery of self-hypnosis.

Progressive Relaxation Induction (PMR—Progressive Muscle Relaxation)

 To start: sit comfortably in a chair, with your feet flat on the floor and your hands on your thighs, not touching. You may also be lying down if that is appropriate. The progressive relaxation induction can take a few minutes to go through, so give yourself some time. It is the staple of hypnotic inductions, though, so it is worth learning, especially for self-hypnosis.

You do not need to memorize the induction. Read through it a few times, practice saying it aloud and you should be ready if you want to record it.

> *Place your feet flat on the floor with your hands on your thighs. Your hands should not touch. Now, take a nice, deep breath, in through the nose and out through the mouth, letting your entire body just relax because it feels good to just let go. Take another deep breath in….and out through the mouth. One final deep breath…in*

through the nose...and let it go Close your eyes down, relaxing completely, feeling comfortable.

Continue to breathe, evenly, steadily, nice deep breaths, knowing that every breath you take relaxes you more, making you feel more comfortable, more secure. As you continue to relax, you may hear other sounds about you...these are just the sounds of everyday living and they only allow you to relax further, feeling more comfortable and more secure.

Now go inside with your eyes closed and pay attention to your toes and feet, noticing how they feel, their weight against the floor, the feeling of your skin...Notice everything you can about how your toes and feet feel....I want you to relax your toes and feet, relaxing every muscle, every nerve and every fiber in your feet and toes, so your toes and feet feel so comfortable, so relaxed, making you feel relaxed and comfortable all over. Count down from 3 to 1 with each number relaxing your toes and feet even more...3....2....1, that's right, excellent, relaxing completely.

Now go deeper inside your mind and focus your attention on your calf muscles, noticing everything about them….how they feel…the sensations in them. Just relax your calves and your shins to the point where they feel so comfortable, so relaxed. The muscles so completely comfortable, so completely relaxed. With every breath you take, relaxing down further, feeling good, feeling secure, going down deeper now. Count you down from 3 to 1 with each number relaxing your calves even more, going deeper now, feeling good….3….2….1, perfect, relaxing down now….feeling good…knowing how good it feels to just relax.

Deeper down now, noticing how relaxed your thighs have already become, and how good it feels to let go, feeling more comfortable as you continue to relax those thighs, those hamstrings, just relaxing more as you continue to take relaxing breaths, breathing in complete relaxations. Count down further from 3 to 1 with each number relaxing your thighs even more, feeling good, comfortable….3….2…1, excellent, you're concentrating perfectly…just letting go, knowing how good it feels to just let go.

Noticing your buttocks now, how comfortably relaxed they has already become, just enjoying that wonderful, peaceful feeling of complete relaxation. All there is, is you. And your quiet comfort now…just let those muscles relax even more, every muscle, every fiber, every nerve, just going down deeper now. That's right…3….2….1…perfect, relaxing perfectly now.

Perhaps you have noticed how comfortable and relaxed your stomach has become, knowing that it feels so good, so secure and so comfortable to just relax even more deeply. There is always another level of relaxation…as you continue to breathe in that relaxation…3…2…1….relaxing perfectly.

You've relaxed perfectly so far, now just completely relax your back as if you're sitting in a comfortable chair, perhaps feeling a warm, tender massage on those muscles, relaxing them even more…3…2…1…letting go, feeling good.

Notice your hands, how they feel at rest, notice how they have relaxed completely. Your whole body relaxing with every breath you take, Yesterday is gone, tomorrow is a million miles *away…all there is, is the here and now and your complete relaxation.*

Your arms becoming completely relaxed, letting that relaxation flow like a gentle stream through your body, your neck and face completely relaxed…feeling good…feeling comfortable…because the deeper you relax the deeper you go and the better you feel. All the way down now, feeling open, ready to accept new and beneficial learnings

This is a version of the progressive relaxation induction (PMR—Progressive Muscle Relaxation). Again, this book is intended to give you some information about hypnosis, not to train you to become a hypnotherapist. If you would like to become a hypnotherapist, the best training available is at Mindworks NLP, at http://www.seattlenlptraining.com.

The specific words of this induction are not crucial. Read through this induction a few times for practice. Coming up, we will give you some hypnotic deepeners that you can use in your self-hypnosis sessions. You can use this technique to take yourself into an even deeper hypnotic state.

When that is done, you will have several of the basic components for self-hypnosis: taking yourself into trance, knowing how to frame suggestions for yourself, delivering suggestions for change and emerging yourself from trance.

Depth of Trance

We often talk about "depth of trance" in hypnosis. "Depth of trance" is usually associated with different hypnotic phenomena that someone can display. Light hypnosis is associated with easy hypnotic phenomena, while deeper levels of trance are associated with hypnotic phenomena generally considered more difficult. For successful unconscious learning/change, depth of trance is not usually the most crucial factor, and significant change work can be done at any level of trance.

The information included here is general information. You obviously will not be able to observe some of these changes as you take yourself into trance. If you eventually decide to take a more complete, live training in hypnosis, then these "signs of trance" will be very useful to you. If you decide to progress towards social (conversational) hypnosis in the future, then these will be of particular benefit. Even in self-hypnosis, you may notice things like lightness or heaviness as you drop into trance.

A simple way to look at depth of trance is by looking at the behavioral and psychological changes that one experiences in different depths of trance. What follows is a standard way of characterizing the different stages of trance.

Stage 1: Light trance. In this state, you feel relaxed and calm. There will be a general, overall relaxation of all the muscle groups, and you may notice the starting of a fixation of attention.

Stage 2: A more relaxed state where muscle groups respond to suggestion. At this stage, your eyes may close. You know you could open them if you wanted to, but they remain comfortably closed. You may notice an increased fixation on some one thing, and your powers of critical thought may go "off line." This is the by-passing of the conscious mind discussed earlier.

Stage 3: You experience a change in major muscle groups. Your hand or arm may remain where it is placed (either with or without suggestion) but will not get tired or feel at all uncomfortable. You can get arm rigidity and other control of major muscle groups. You may start feeling analgesia (pain control). On suggestion, there may be amnesia of numbers or other items.

Stage 4: This is a deeper stage, and suggestion may create amnesia for your name, numbers and other things. Analgesia is more common here. There may be time distortion, and a half hour of hypnosis may seem like only five minutes or so.

Stage 5: This is a state called somnambulism and is usually the state a client will go into when using hypnotherapy. It can easily be achieved in self-hypnosis as well. Many techniques of pain control are effective at this depth of hypnosis. If suggested to you, you may experience positive hallucinations (seeing things that are not there) or negative hallucinations (failing to see things that are there). At this stage, you may also experience age regression. In some charts, you may see positive and negative hallucinations in separate stages; we are only giving a general statement about depth of trance here.

Stage 6: This is the so-called "hypnotic coma," and is perhaps the deepest stage of hypnosis.

Deepeners

After you've gone into trance, it is sometimes useful to deepen the trance to the point where your suggestions will take root and be the most effective. Deepeners are ways of taking a level of trance and making it deeper. Some hypnotists think that more effective change work is done at the deeper levels of trance—and for some things, such a pain control, it is probably advisable. Listed below are some common deepeners.

Breath Deepener

There are a number of easy and effective ways to deepen your trance state. One way is to connect your breathing with depth of trance: "As I continue to breathe deeply and evenly I go deeper into this wonderful state of hypnotic relaxation, allowing my unconscious mind to bring me that perfect level of trance for these changes."

Staircase Deepener

 Another way to deepen trance is to connect the level of trance with specific kinds of images. For example, you might imagine yourself at the

top of a staircase. As you walk down that staircase, with each step you go deeper and deeper into trance. When you reach the bottom, you are at the perfect level of trance for the change work you want to make. Let yourself walk down without consciously thinking of the steps. Just set the scenario, and let your unconscious mind take over from there.

Elevator Deepener

Like the staircase deepener, with the elevator deepener, you imagine yourself riding down an elevator. As the elevator moves down from the 20th floor to the 19th floor to the 18th floor, and so on, you drop deeper and deeper into hypnotic trance.

Floating Feather Deepener

Imagine a feather floating, fluttering down from the sky, gentle swaying in air. As the feather floats down to the ground, you go deeper and deeper into a state of wonderful hypnotic trance. It is a relaxing image, a lazy image, as you imaging the feather floating down and when it finally reaches the ground, your unconscious mind is at that perfect place to accept positive suggestions.

The Need for Deepeners

After you have gone through a few self-hypnosis sessions, you will likely not find any need for deepeners. You will quickly go into a good level of trance, necessary for the changes that you want to make, and the need for these deepeners will probably no longer be necessary. And when they are no longer necessary, of course, you can omit them from your self-hypnosis.

If you decide to take your hypnosis skills to the next level and start hypnotizing others, then these deepeners will be quite useful.

In this section, you learned about the mind/body connection, and we illustrated the connection with the pendulum exercise. In fact, you can use the mind/body connection to change your state of mind when you are not feeling the way you want to. Just think how someone would hold their body when they feel the way you want to feel, and then hold your own body in that way. You will notice that your mental state changes very quickly. Feeling depressed? Hold your body upright, shoulders back, put a smile on your face, and watch the old feeling disappear into something new.

You also learned about the signs of trance, and how to deepen trance.

You also learned a couple of standard inductions—the Progressive Muscle Relaxation (PMR) and the Betty Erickson Induction. We encourage you to play with everything you've learned about self-hypnosis, and to keep learning.

Chapter 5: Conclusion

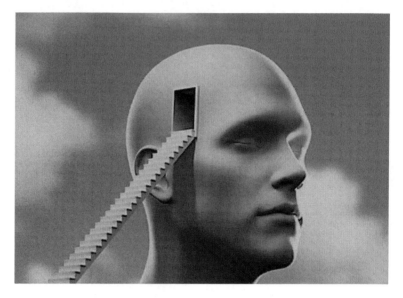

I hope you have enjoyed reading about hypnosis and have come to understand some of the power of your unconscious mind in everything you do. You can improve almost every aspect of your life, from habits, to beliefs, to attitudes, to self-perception to any skill you want to develop through hypnosis. Hypnosis has been used for at least 2,000 years to help people achieve heath, wealth and wisdom. Be part of that change as you continue to improve your life.

You have learned in this book some basic facts about hypnosis, have discovered the truth about hypnosis vs. the myths of hypnosis. You learned about goal setting and how to form suggestions for change. You have learned how to take yourself into a deep hypnotic state and how to use hypnosis to make significant changes in your own life.

Here is a summary of the process for self-hypnosis as well as the process for using the audio to take yourself into hypnotic trance.

The Process to date:

Preparation Steps:

1. Get Comfortable
2. Decide on a length of time for hypnosis
3. Say how you want to feel when you come out of trance
4. State your goal for the hypnotic session.
5. State what you want (the suggestion for this particular hypnotic trance)

The Induction

6. Use one of the techniques for self-hypnosis revealed in this book
7. Use one of the deepeners in this book if desired.

8. Let your mind drift as your unconscious activates the suggestion

Emerge

9. Emerge from trance feeling the way you instructed yourself to feel knowing that the suggestion you gave yourself is already taking deep root in your mind.

The audio CD:

 We are offering an audio file to take you into trance and give you a trigger word for going into a deep trance instantly. You can download the audio file at:

http://www.hypnosistraininglab.com/selfhypnosisaudio cd

The instructions for using the CD are located there as well.

The key phrase is "relaxing now," and the phrase will only take you into hypnosis when you have a positive desire to go into hypnosis. When you use that phrase to go into trance, make sure you are in a comfortable, safe place where you will not be disturbed for the duration of the session. You will always, of course, immediately emerge from trance if there is some emergency requiring your attention.

Once you are ready to go into trance, simply say the trigger word to yourself at step 6 of the process laid out above.

A Final Note

Hypnosis is a fascinating field and I hope this book has given you an insight into the many possibilities.

As your interest in hypnosis continues to grow, you will always be able to find more information about hypnosis at:

https://www.hypnosistraininglab.com

https://www.mindworkshypnosis.net

https://www.seattlenlptraining.com

If you have any questions about hypnosis or comments on this book, please email me at:

beyondtheconsciousmind@hypnosistraininglab.com

May your unconscious mind always guide you to new power, joy and self-fulfillment!

Made in the USA
Middletown, DE
12 April 2021